THE**ACTIVATOR**

Listen. We know you don't have time for all those confusing conversations and emotions that get in the way of just getting stuff done! But maximum achievement is severly hindered when you completely rule out emotions, or overload yourself, especially with tasks and expectations that aren't even yours!

Enter, the Activator.

We hope this planner will maximize your performance by helping clarify your own expectations of success, strengthen your relationships, strategize where your time and energy go (sadly, it IS limited superhero), and getting ahead of blind-spots that would ultimately hold you back from full velocity.

So...what do YOU want to activate today?!

MONTH:

MONDAY	TUESDAY	WEDNESDAY	THURSDAY	FRIDAY	SATURDAY	SUNDAY

MONTH:

MONDAY	TUESDAY	WEDNESDAY	THURSDAY	FRIDAY	SATURDAY	SUNDAY

MONTH:

MONDAY	TUESDAY	WEDNESDAY	THURSDAY	FRIDAY	SATURDAY	SUNDAY

EXAMPLE PAGE

DATE

QUARTERLY FOCUS:

YOU ARE MORE THAN WHAT YOU DO
You are LOVED for **who you are** not what you do

Getting elected to City Council

WEEKLY SNAPSHOT:

MON	TUE	WED	THU	FRI	SAT	SUN
Big meeting Game	*Project*	*Project*	*Project*	*File for Election*	*Date night*	*Competition*

IT'S OKAY TO DO THINGS 80%

TODAY'S OBJECTIVES

1 PROJECT / GOAL *Work*

Get final approvals and finalize details for Hansen Project

SPECIFIC TASKS

Meeting with Carl
Finalize building plans
Approval on location
Order Supplies

2 PROJECT / GOAL *Family*

Coach Timmy's baseball game

SPECIFIC TASKS

Pick up the gear
Remind Jay about snacks
Parents sign-up sheet
Oil Timmy's mitt

3 PROJECT / GOAL *Crossfit Prep*

Train for Competition Saturday

SPECIFIC TASKS

Warm-ups
1 Hr legs
30 oz of water
Protein Shake
Stretches

Which tasks are not necessary for me to do?
Which tasks can be delegated?
I could delegate the ordering of supplies to Sam...

What does success look like to me? If I step back from the expectations of others, what do I actually want to do today?
Success looks like... being a wife and mom that is present, and making a positive impact on my community...

YESTERDAY'S WIN:

Added 2.5 lbs to my leg workout!

It's okay to celebrate even the simple wins!

M O T I V E S
C H E C K

You don't have to be "silent" or "motionless" to have space to think. An activity that still allows for brain space is perfect.

Where is the space this week for contemplation?

DAY(S): *M - T - W*
TIME: *6am*
ACTIVITY:
  - *in the shower*
  - *camping trip*
  - *walking the dog*
  - *painting*

DATE

QUARTERLY FOCUS:

WEEKLY SNAPSHOT:

MON	TUE	WED	THU	FRI	SAT	SUN

IT'S OKAY TO DO THINGS 80%

T O D A Y ' S
O B J E C T I V E S

1 PROJECT / GOAL

SPECIFIC **TASKS**

2 PROJECT / GOAL

SPECIFIC **TASKS**

3 PROJECT / GOAL

SPECIFIC **TASKS**

Which tasks are not necessary for me to do?
Which tasks can be delegated?"

_____

_____

_____

_____

What does success look like to me? If I step back from the
expectations of others, what do I actually want to do today?

_____

_____

YESTERDAY'S WIN:

M O T I V E S
C H E C K

What can I do
today and not
take credit for?

Where is the space
this week for
contemplation?

DAY(S):
TIME:
ACTIVITY:

DATE
QUARTERLY FOCUS:

YOU ARE MORE THAN WHAT YOU DO
You are LOVED for **who you are** not what you do

WEEKLY SNAPSHOT:

MON	TUE	WED	THU	FRI	SAT	SUN

IT'S OKAY TO DO THINGS 80%

TODAY'S OBJECTIVES

1 PROJECT / GOAL	SPECIFIC **TASKS**

2 PROJECT / GOAL	SPECIFIC **TASKS**

3 PROJECT / GOAL	SPECIFIC **TASKS**

Which tasks are not necessary for me to do?
Which tasks can be delegated?"

_____

_____

_____

What does success look like to me? If I step back from the
expectations of others, what do I actually want to do today?

_____

_____

YESTERDAY'S WIN:

**M O T I V E S
C H E C K**

What can I do
today and not
take credit for?

Where is the space
this week for
contemplation?

DAY(S):
TIME:
ACTIVITY:

DATE
QUARTERLY FOCUS:

WEEKLY SNAPSHOT:

MON	TUE	WED	THU	FRI	SAT	SUN

IT'S OKAY TO DO THINGS 80%

T O D A Y ' S
O B J E C T I V E S

1 PROJECT / GOAL

SPECIFIC **TASKS**

2 PROJECT / GOAL

SPECIFIC **TASKS**

3 PROJECT / GOAL

SPECIFIC **TASKS**

Which tasks are not necessary for me to do?
Which tasks can be delegated?"

_____

_____

_____

What does success look like to me? If I step back from the
expectations of others, what do I actually want to do today?

_____

_____

YESTERDAY'S WIN:

M O T I V E S
C H E C K

What can I do
today and not
take credit for?

Where is the space
this week for
contemplation?

DAY(S):
TIME:
ACTIVITY:

DATE
QUARTERLY FOCUS:

YOU ARE MORE THAN WHAT YOU DO
You are LOVED for **who you are** not what you do

WEEKLY SNAPSHOT:

MON	TUE	WED	THU	FRI	SAT	SUN

IT'S OKAY TO DO THINGS 80%

TODAY'S OBJECTIVES

1 PROJECT / GOAL	SPECIFIC **TASKS**

2 PROJECT / GOAL	SPECIFIC **TASKS**

3 PROJECT / GOAL	SPECIFIC **TASKS**

Which tasks are not necessary for me to do?
Which tasks can be delegated?"

_____

_____

_____

What does success look like to me? If I step back from the
expectations of others, what do I actually want to do today?

_____

_____

YESTERDAY'S WIN:

**M O T I V E S
C H E C K**

What can I do
today and not
take credit for?

Where is the space
this week for
contemplation?

DAY(S):
TIME:
ACTIVITY:

DATE
QUARTERLY FOCUS:

WEEKLY SNAPSHOT:

MON	TUE	WED	THU	FRI	SAT	SUN

IT'S OKAY TO DO THINGS 80%

**T O D A Y ' S
O B J E C T I V E S**

1 PROJECT / GOAL	SPECIFIC **TASKS**

2 PROJECT / GOAL	SPECIFIC **TASKS**

3 PROJECT / GOAL	SPECIFIC **TASKS**

Which tasks are not necessary for me to do?
Which tasks can be delegated?"

_____

_____

_____

What does success look like to me? If I step back from the
expectations of others, what do I actually want to do today?

_____

_____

YESTERDAY'S WIN:

**M O T I V E S
C H E C K**

What can I do
today and not
take credit for?

Where is the space
this week for
contemplation?

DAY(S):
TIME:
ACTIVITY:

DATE
QUARTERLY FOCUS:

WEEKLY SNAPSHOT:

MON	TUE	WED	THU	FRI	SAT	SUN

IT'S OKAY TO DO THINGS 80%

TODAY'S OBJECTIVES

1 PROJECT / GOAL	SPECIFIC TASKS

2 PROJECT / GOAL	SPECIFIC TASKS

3 PROJECT / GOAL	SPECIFIC TASKS

Which tasks are not necessary for me to do?
Which tasks can be delegated?"

_____

_____

_____

What does success look like to me? If I step back from the
expectations of others, what do I actually want to do today?

_____

_____

YESTERDAY'S WIN:

**M O T I V E S
C H E C K**

What can I do
today and not
take credit for?

Where is the space
this week for
contemplation?

DAY(S):
TIME:
ACTIVITY:

DATE
QUARTERLY FOCUS:

YOU ARE MORE THAN WHAT YOU DO
You are LOVED for **who you are** not what you do

WEEKLY SNAPSHOT:

MON	TUE	WED	THU	FRI	SAT	SUN

IT'S OKAY TO DO THINGS 80%

T O D A Y ' S
O B J E C T I V E S

1 PROJECT / GOAL	SPECIFIC **TASKS**

2 PROJECT / GOAL	SPECIFIC **TASKS**

3 PROJECT / GOAL	SPECIFIC **TASKS**

Which tasks are not necessary for me to do?
Which tasks can be delegated?"

_____

_____

_____

What does success look like to me? If I step back from the
expectations of others, what do I actually want to do today?

_____

_____

YESTERDAY'S WIN:

M O T I V E S
C H E C K

What can I do
today and not
take credit for?

Where is the space
this week for
contemplation?

DAY(S):
TIME:
ACTIVITY:

DATE
QUARTERLY FOCUS:

YOU ARE MORE THAN WHAT YOU DO
You are LOVED for **who you are** not what you do

WEEKLY SNAPSHOT:

MON	TUE	WED	THU	FRI	SAT	SUN

IT'S OKAY TO DO THINGS 80%

TODAY'S OBJECTIVES

1 PROJECT / GOAL	SPECIFIC TASKS

2 PROJECT / GOAL	SPECIFIC TASKS

3 PROJECT / GOAL	SPECIFIC TASKS

Which tasks are not necessary for me to do?
Which tasks can be delegated?"

_____
_____
_____
_____

What does success look like to me? If I step back from the
expectations of others, what do I actually want to do today?

_____
_____

YESTERDAY'S WIN:

MOTIVES
CHECK

What can I do
today and not
take credit for?

Where is the space
this week for
contemplation?

DAY(S):
TIME:
ACTIVITY:

DATE
QUARTERLY FOCUS:

YOU ARE MORE THAN WHAT YOU DO
You are LOVED for **who you are** not what you do

WEEKLY SNAPSHOT:

MON	TUE	WED	THU	FRI	SAT	SUN

IT'S OKAY TO DO THINGS 80%

T O D A Y ' S
O B J E C T I V E S

1 PROJECT / GOAL	SPECIFIC **TASKS**

2 PROJECT / GOAL	SPECIFIC **TASKS**

3 PROJECT / GOAL	SPECIFIC **TASKS**

Which tasks are not necessary for me to do?
Which tasks can be delegated?"

_____

_____

_____

What does success look like to me? If I step back from the
expectations of others, what do I actually want to do today?

_____

_____

YESTERDAY'S WIN:

M O T I V E S
C H E C K

What can I do
today and not
take credit for?

Where is the space
this week for
contemplation?

DAY(S):
TIME:
ACTIVITY:

DATE

QUARTERLY FOCUS:

YOU ARE MORE THAN WHAT YOU DO
You are LOVED for **who you are** not what you do

WEEKLY SNAPSHOT:

MON	TUE	WED	THU	FRI	SAT	SUN

IT'S OKAY TO DO THINGS 80%

TODAY'S OBJECTIVES

1 PROJECT / GOAL	SPECIFIC **TASKS**

2 PROJECT / GOAL	SPECIFIC **TASKS**

3 PROJECT / GOAL	SPECIFIC **TASKS**

Which tasks are not necessary for me to do?
Which tasks can be delegated?"

_____
_____
_____

What does success look like to me? If I step back from the expectations of others, what do I actually want to do today?

_____
_____

YESTERDAY'S WIN:

**M O T I V E S
C H E C K**

What can I do today and not take credit for?

Where is the space this week for contemplation?

DAY(S):
TIME:
ACTIVITY:

DATE
QUARTERLY FOCUS:

WEEKLY SNAPSHOT:

MON	TUE	WED	THU	FRI	SAT	SUN

IT'S OKAY TO DO THINGS 80%

**T O D A Y ' S
O B J E C T I V E S**

1 PROJECT / GOAL	SPECIFIC **TASKS**

2 PROJECT / GOAL	SPECIFIC **TASKS**

3 PROJECT / GOAL	SPECIFIC **TASKS**

Which tasks are not necessary for me to do?
Which tasks can be delegated?"

_____

_____

_____

What does success look like to me? If I step back from the
expectations of others, what do I actually want to do today?

_____

_____

YESTERDAY'S WIN:

**M O T I V E S
C H E C K**

What can I do
today and not
take credit for?

Where is the space
this week for
contemplation?

DAY(S):
TIME:
ACTIVITY:

DATE
QUARTERLY FOCUS:

YOU ARE MORE THAN WHAT YOU DO
You are LOVED for **who you are** not what you do

WEEKLY SNAPSHOT·

MON	TUE	WED	THU	FRI	SAT	SUN

IT'S OKAY TO DO THINGS 80%

TODAY'S OBJECTIVES

1 PROJECT / GOAL

SPECIFIC **TASKS**

2 PROJECT / GOAL

SPECIFIC **TASKS**

3 PROJECT / GOAL

SPECIFIC **TASKS**

Which tasks are not necessary for me to do?
Which tasks can be delegated?"

_____

_____

_____

_____

What does success look like to me? If I step back from the
expectations of others, what do I actually want to do today?

_____

_____

YESTERDAY'S WIN:

MOTIVES CHECK

What can I do
today and not
take credit for?

Where is the space
this week for
contemplation?

DAY(S):
TIME:
ACTIVITY:

DATE

QUARTERLY FOCUS:

WEEKLY SNAPSHOT:

MON	TUE	WED	THU	FRI	SAT	SUN

IT'S OKAY TO DO THINGS 80%

T O D A Y ' S
O B J E C T I V E S

1 PROJECT / GOAL	SPECIFIC **TASKS**

2 PROJECT / GOAL	SPECIFIC **TASKS**

3 PROJECT / GOAL	SPECIFIC **TASKS**

Which tasks are not necessary for me to do?
Which tasks can be delegated?"

_____

_____

_____

What does success look like to me? If I step back from the
expectations of others, what do I actually want to do today?

_____

_____

YESTERDAY'S WIN:

M O T I V E S
C H E C K

What can I do
today and not
take credit for?

Where is the space
this week for
contemplation?

DAY(S):
TIME:
ACTIVITY:

DATE
QUARTERLY FOCUS:

WEEKLY SNAPSHOT:

MON	TUE	WED	THU	FRI	SAT	SUN

IT'S OKAY TO DO THINGS **80%** **TODAY'S** OBJECTIVES

1 **PROJECT /** GOAL	SPECIFIC **TASKS**

2 **PROJECT /** GOAL	SPECIFIC **TASKS**

3 **PROJECT /** GOAL	SPECIFIC **TASKS**

Which tasks are not necessary for me to do?
Which tasks can be delegated?"

_____

_____

_____

What does success look like to me? If I step back from the
expectations of others, what do I actually want to do today?

_____

_____

YESTERDAY'S WIN:

**M O T I V E S
C H E C K**

What can I do
today and not
take credit for?

Where is the space
this week for
contemplation?

DAY(S):
TIME:
ACTIVITY:

DATE

QUARTERLY FOCUS:

YOU ARE MORE THAN WHAT YOU DO
You are LOVED for **who you are** not what you do

WEEKLY SNAPSHOT:

MON	TUE	WED	THU	FRI	SAT	SUN

IT'S   OKAY   TO   DO   THINGS   **80%**

T O D A Y ' S
O B J E C T I V E S

1 PROJECT / GOAL

SPECIFIC **TASKS**

2 PROJECT / GOAL

SPECIFIC **TASKS**

3 PROJECT / GOAL

SPECIFIC **TASKS**

Which tasks are not necessary for me to do?
Which tasks can be delegated?"

_____

_____

_____

What does success look like to me? If I step back from the
expectations of others, what do I actually want to do today?

_____

_____

YESTERDAY'S WIN:

M O T I V E S
C H E C K

What can I do
today and not
take credit for?

Where is the space
this week for
contemplation?

DAY(S):
TIME:
ACTIVITY:

DATE
QUARTERLY FOCUS:

WEEKLY SNAPSHOT:

MON	TUE	WED	THU	FRI	SAT	SUN

IT'S OKAY TO DO THINGS 80%

TODAY'S OBJECTIVES

1 PROJECT / GOAL	SPECIFIC **TASKS**

2 PROJECT / GOAL	SPECIFIC **TASKS**

3 PROJECT / GOAL	SPECIFIC **TASKS**

Which tasks are not necessary for me to do?
Which tasks can be delegated?"

_____

_____

_____

What does success look like to me? If I step back from the
expectations of others, what do I actually want to do today?

_____

_____

YESTERDAY'S WIN:

M O T I V E S
C H E C K

What can I do
today and not
take credit for?

Where is the space
this week for
contemplation?

DAY(S):
TIME:
ACTIVITY:

DATE
QUARTERLY FOCUS:

YOU ARE MORE THAN WHAT YOU DO
You are LOVED for **who you are** not what you do

WEEKLY SNAPSHOT:

MON	TUE	WED	THU	FRI	SAT	SUN

IT'S OKAY TO DO THINGS 80%

T O D A Y ' S
O B J E C T I V E S

1 **PROJECT /** GOAL	SPECIFIC **TASKS**

2 **PROJECT /** GOAL	SPECIFIC **TASKS**

3 **PROJECT /** GOAL	SPECIFIC **TASKS**

Which tasks are not necessary for me to do?
Which tasks can be delegated?"

_____
_____
_____

What does success look like to me? If I step back from the
expectations of others, what do I actually want to do today?

_____
_____

YESTERDAY'S WIN:

M O T I V E S
C H E C K

What can I do
today and not
take credit for?

Where is the space
this week for
contemplation?

DAY(S):
TIME:
ACTIVITY:

DATE
QUARTERLY FOCUS:

WEEKLY SNAPSHOT:

MON	TUE	WED	THU	FRI	SAT	SUN

IT'S OKAY TO DO THINGS 80%

TODAY'S OBJECTIVES

1 PROJECT / GOAL	SPECIFIC **TASKS**

2 PROJECT / GOAL	SPECIFIC **TASKS**

3 PROJECT / GOAL	SPECIFIC **TASKS**

Which tasks are not necessary for me to do?
Which tasks can be delegated?"

_____

_____

_____

What does success look like to me? If I step back from the
expectations of others, what do I actually want to do today?

_____

_____

YESTERDAY'S WIN:

**M O T I V E S
C H E C K**

What can I do
today and not
take credit for?

Where is the space
this week for
contemplation?

DAY(S):
TIME:
ACTIVITY:

DATE
QUARTERLY FOCUS:

WEEKLY SNAPSHOT:

MON	TUE	WED	THU	FRI	SAT	SUN

IT'S OKAY TO DO THINGS **80%**

T O D A Y ' S
O B J E C T I V E S

1 PROJECT / GOAL		SPECIFIC **TASKS**

2 PROJECT / GOAL		SPECIFIC **TASKS**

3 PROJECT / GOAL		SPECIFIC **TASKS**

Which tasks are not necessary for me to do?
Which tasks can be delegated?"

_____
_____
_____
_____

What does success look like to me? If I step back from the
expectations of others, what do I actually want to do today?

_____
_____

YESTERDAY'S WIN:

M O T I V E S
C H E C K

What can I do
today and not
take credit for?

Where is the space
this week for
contemplation?

DAY(S):
TIME:
ACTIVITY:

DATE
QUARTERLY FOCUS:

YOU ARE MORE THAN WHAT YOU DO
You are LOVED for **who you are** not what you do

WEEKLY SNAPSHOT:

MON	TUE	WED	THU	FRI	SAT	SUN

IT'S OKAY TO DO THINGS 80%

TODAY'S OBJECTIVES

1 PROJECT / GOAL	SPECIFIC **TASKS**

2 PROJECT / GOAL	SPECIFIC **TASKS**

3 PROJECT / GOAL	SPECIFIC **TASKS**

Which tasks are not necessary for me to do?
Which tasks can be delegated?"

_____

_____

_____

What does success look like to me? If I step back from the
expectations of others, what do I actually want to do today?

_____

_____

YESTERDAY'S WIN:

M O T I V E S
C H E C K

What can I do
today and not
take credit for?

Where is the space
this week for
contemplation?

DAY(S):
TIME:
ACTIVITY:

DATE
QUARTERLY FOCUS:

WEEKLY SNAPSHOT:

MON	TUE	WED	THU	FRI	SAT	SUN

IT'S OKAY TO DO THINGS 80%

TODAY'S OBJECTIVES

1 PROJECT / GOAL

SPECIFIC **TASKS**

2 PROJECT / GOAL

SPECIFIC **TASKS**

3 PROJECT / GOAL

SPECIFIC **TASKS**

Which tasks are not necessary for me to do?
Which tasks can be delegated?"

_____

_____

_____

What does success look like to me? If I step back from the
expectations of others, what do I actually want to do today?

_____

_____

YESTERDAY'S WIN:

MOTIVES CHECK

What can I do
today and not
take credit for?

Where is the space
this week for
contemplation?

DAY(S):
TIME:
ACTIVITY:

DATE
QUARTERLY FOCUS:

YOU ARE MORE THAN WHAT YOU DO
You are LOVED for **who you are** not what you do

WEEKLY SNAPSHOT:

MON	TUE	WED	THU	FRI	SAT	SUN

IT'S OKAY TO DO THINGS 80%

TODAY'S OBJECTIVES

1 PROJECT / GOAL	SPECIFIC **TASKS**

2 PROJECT / GOAL	SPECIFIC **TASKS**

3 PROJECT / GOAL	SPECIFIC **TASKS**

Which tasks are not necessary for me to do?
Which tasks can be delegated?"

_____

_____

_____

What does success look like to me? If I step back from the
expectations of others, what do I actually want to do today?

_____

_____

YESTERDAY'S WIN:

MOTIVES CHECK

What can I do
today and not
take credit for?

Where is the space
this week for
contemplation?

DAY(S):
TIME:
ACTIVITY:

DATE
QUARTERLY FOCUS:

WEEKLY SNAPSHOT:

MON	TUE	WED	THU	FRI	SAT	SUN

IT'S OKAY TO DO THINGS 80%

T O D A Y ' S
O B J E C T I V E S

1 PROJECT / GOAL	SPECIFIC **TASKS**

2 PROJECT / GOAL	SPECIFIC **TASKS**

3 PROJECT / GOAL	SPECIFIC **TASKS**

Which tasks are not necessary for me to do?
Which tasks can be delegated?"

_____

_____

_____

What does success look like to me? If I step back from the
expectations of others, what do I actually want to do today?

_____

_____

YESTERDAY'S WIN:

M O T I V E S
C H E C K

What can I do
today and not
take credit for?

Where is the space
this week for
contemplation?

DAY(S):
TIME:
ACTIVITY:

DATE
QUARTERLY FOCUS:

YOU ARE MORE THAN WHAT YOU DO
You are LOVED for **who you are** not what you do

WEEKLY SNAPSHOT:

MON	TUE	WED	THU	FRI	SAT	SUN

IT'S OKAY TO DO THINGS 80%

TODAY'S OBJECTIVES

1 PROJECT / GOAL	SPECIFIC **TASKS**

2 PROJECT / GOAL	SPECIFIC **TASKS**

3 PROJECT / GOAL	SPECIFIC **TASKS**

Which tasks are not necessary for me to do?
Which tasks can be delegated?"

_____

_____

_____

What does success look like to me? If I step back from the
expectations of others, what do I actually want to do today?

_____

_____

YESTERDAY'S WIN:

M O T I V E S
C H E C K

What can I do
today and not
take credit for?

Where is the space
this week for
contemplation?

DAY(S):
TIME:
ACTIVITY:

DATE
QUARTERLY FOCUS:

WEEKLY SNAPSHOT:

MON	TUE	WED	THU	FRI	SAT	SUN

IT'S OKAY TO DO THINGS 80%

T O D A Y ' S
O B J E C T I V E S

1 PROJECT / GOAL	SPECIFIC **TASKS**

2 PROJECT / GOAL	SPECIFIC **TASKS**

3 PROJECT / GOAL	SPECIFIC **TASKS**

Which tasks are not necessary for me to do?
Which tasks can be delegated?"

_____

_____

_____

What does success look like to me? If I step back from the
expectations of others, what do I actually want to do today?

_____

_____

YESTERDAY'S WIN:

M O T I V E S
C H E C K

What can I do
today and not
take credit for?

Where is the space
this week for
contemplation?

DAY(S):
TIME:
ACTIVITY:

DATE
QUARTERLY FOCUS:

WEEKLY SNAPSHOT:

MON	TUE	WED	THU	FRI	SAT	SUN

IT'S OKAY TO DO THINGS 80%   **TODAY'S** OBJECTIVES

1 PROJECT / GOAL	SPECIFIC **TASKS**

2 PROJECT / GOAL	SPECIFIC **TASKS**

3 PROJECT / GOAL	SPECIFIC **TASKS**

Which tasks are not necessary for me to do?
Which tasks can be delegated?"

_____

_____

_____

What does success look like to me? If I step back from the
expectations of others, what do I actually want to do today?

_____

_____

YESTERDAY'S WIN:

M O T I V E S
C H E C K

What can I do
today and not
take credit for?

Where is the space
this week for
contemplation?

DAY(S):
TIME:
ACTIVITY:

DATE
QUARTERLY FOCUS:

YOU ARE MORE THAN WHAT YOU DO
You are LOVED for **who you are** not what you do

WEEKLY SNAPSHOT:

MON	TUE	WED	THU	FRI	SAT	SUN

IT'S OKAY TO DO THINGS **80%**

TODAY'S OBJECTIVES

1 PROJECT / GOAL

SPECIFIC **TASKS**

2 PROJECT / GOAL

SPECIFIC **TASKS**

3 PROJECT / GOAL

SPECIFIC **TASKS**

Which tasks are not necessary for me to do?
Which tasks can be delegated?"

_____

_____

_____

What does success look like to me? If I step back from the
expectations of others, what do I actually want to do today?

_____

_____

YESTERDAY'S WIN:

MOTIVES CHECK

What can I do
today and not
take credit for?

Where is the space
this week for
contemplation?

DAY(S):
TIME:
ACTIVITY:

DATE
QUARTERLY FOCUS:

YOU ARE MORE THAN WHAT YOU DO
You are LOVED for **who you are** not what you do

WEEKLY SNAPSHOT:

MON	TUE	WED	THU	FRI	SAT	SUN

IT'S OKAY TO DO THINGS 80%

TODAY'S OBJECTIVES

1 **PROJECT** / GOAL	SPECIFIC **TASKS**

2 **PROJECT** / GOAL	SPECIFIC **TASKS**

3 **PROJECT** / GOAL	SPECIFIC **TASKS**

Which tasks are not necessary for me to do?
Which tasks can be delegated?"

_____

_____

_____

What does success look like to me? If I step back from the
expectations of others, what do I actually want to do today?

_____

_____

YESTERDAY'S WIN:

MOTIVES CHECK

What can I do
today and not
take credit for?

Where is the space
this week for
contemplation?

DAY(S):
TIME:
ACTIVITY:

DATE
QUARTERLY FOCUS:

WEEKLY SNAPSHOT:

MON	TUE	WED	THU	FRI	SAT	SUN

IT'S OKAY TO DO THINGS 80%

TODAY'S OBJECTIVES

1 **PROJECT** / GOAL	SPECIFIC **TASKS**

2 **PROJECT** / GOAL	SPECIFIC **TASKS**

3 **PROJECT** / GOAL	SPECIFIC **TASKS**

Which tasks are not necessary for me to do?
Which tasks can be delegated?"

_____

_____

_____

What does success look like to me? If I step back from the
expectations of others, what do I actually want to do today?

_____

_____

YESTERDAY'S WIN:

**M O T I V E S
C H E C K**

What can I do
today and not
take credit for?

Where is the space
this week for
contemplation?

DAY(S):
TIME:
ACTIVITY:

DATE
QUARTERLY FOCUS:

YOU ARE MORE THAN WHAT YOU DO
You are LOVED for **who you are** not what you do

WEEKLY SNAPSHOT:

MON	TUE	WED	THU	FRI	SAT	SUN

IT'S OKAY TO DO THINGS 80%   **TODAY'S** OBJECTIVES

1 **PROJECT** / GOAL	SPECIFIC **TASKS**

2 **PROJECT** / GOAL	SPECIFIC **TASKS**

3 **PROJECT** / GOAL	SPECIFIC **TASKS**

Which tasks are not necessary for me to do?
Which tasks can be delegated?"

_____

_____

_____

What does success look like to me? If I step back from the
expectations of others, what do I actually want to do today?

_____

_____

YESTERDAY'S WIN:

MOTIVES CHECK

What can I do
today and not
take credit for?

Where is the space
this week for
contemplation?

DAY(S):
TIME:
ACTIVITY:

DATE
QUARTERLY FOCUS:

YOU ARE MORE THAN WHAT YOU DO
You are LOVED for **who you are** not what you do

WEEKLY SNAPSHOT:

MON	TUE	WED	THU	FRI	SAT	SUN

IT'S OKAY TO DO THINGS 80%

TODAY'S OBJECTIVES

1 PROJECT / GOAL	SPECIFIC **TASKS**

2 PROJECT / GOAL	SPECIFIC **TASKS**

3 PROJECT / GOAL	SPECIFIC **TASKS**

Which tasks are not necessary for me to do?
Which tasks can be delegated?"

_____

_____

_____

What does success look like to me? If I step back from the
expectations of others, what do I actually want to do today?

_____

_____

YESTERDAY'S WIN:

MOTIVES CHECK

What can I do
today and not
take credit for?

Where is the space
this week for
contemplation?

DAY(S):
TIME:
ACTIVITY:

DATE
QUARTERLY FOCUS:

WEEKLY SNAPSHOT:

MON	TUE	WED	THU	FRI	SAT	SUN

IT'S OKAY TO DO THINGS 80%

TODAY'S OBJECTIVES

1 **PROJECT** / GOAL	SPECIFIC **TASKS**

2 **PROJECT** / GOAL	SPECIFIC **TASKS**

3 **PROJECT** / GOAL	SPECIFIC **TASKS**

Which tasks are not necessary for me to do?
Which tasks can be delegated?"

_____

_____

_____

_____

What does success look like to me? If I step back from the
expectations of others, what do I actually want to do today?

_____

_____

YESTERDAY'S WIN:

M O T I V E S
C H E C K

What can I do
today and not
take credit for?

Where is the space
this week for
contemplation?

DAY(S):
TIME:
ACTIVITY:

DATE
QUARTERLY FOCUS:

WEEKLY SNAPSHOT:

MON	TUE	WED	THU	FRI	SAT	SUN

IT'S OKAY TO DO THINGS 80%

**T O D A Y ' S
O B J E C T I V E S**

1 PROJECT / GOAL	SPECIFIC **TASKS**

2 PROJECT / GOAL	SPECIFIC **TASKS**

3 PROJECT / GOAL	SPECIFIC **TASKS**

Which tasks are not necessary for me to do?
Which tasks can be delegated?"

_____

_____

_____

What does success look like to me? If I step back from the
expectations of others, what do I actually want to do today?

_____

_____

YESTERDAY'S WIN:

**M O T I V E S
C H E C K**

What can I do
today and not
take credit for?

Where is the space
this week for
contemplation?

DAY(S):
TIME:
ACTIVITY:

DATE
QUARTERLY FOCUS:

YOU ARE MORE THAN WHAT YOU DO
You are LOVED for **who you are** not what you do

WEEKLY SNAPSHOT:

MON	TUE	WED	THU	FRI	SAT	SUN

IT'S OKAY TO DO THINGS 80%

TODAY'S OBJECTIVES

1 PROJECT / GOAL	SPECIFIC TASKS

2 PROJECT / GOAL	SPECIFIC TASKS

3 PROJECT / GOAL	SPECIFIC TASKS

Which tasks are not necessary for me to do?
Which tasks can be delegated?"

_____

_____

_____

What does success look like to me? If I step back from the
expectations of others, what do I actually want to do today?

_____

_____

YESTERDAY'S WIN:

**M O T I V E S
C H E C K**

What can I do
today and not
take credit for?

Where is the space
this week for
contemplation?

DAY(S):
TIME:
ACTIVITY:

DATE
QUARTERLY FOCUS:

YOU ARE MORE THAN WHAT YOU DO
You are LOVED for **who you are** not what you do

WEEKLY SNAPSHOT:

MON	TUE	WED	THU	FRI	SAT	SUN

IT'S OKAY TO DO THINGS 80%

TODAY'S OBJECTIVES

1 **PROJECT /** GOAL	SPECIFIC **TASKS**

2 **PROJECT /** GOAL	SPECIFIC **TASKS**

3 **PROJECT /** GOAL	SPECIFIC **TASKS**

Which tasks are not necessary for me to do?
Which tasks can be delegated?"

_____
_____
_____

What does success look like to me? If I step back from the
expectations of others, what do I actually want to do today?

_____
_____

YESTERDAY'S WIN:

MOTIVES CHECK

What can I do
today and not
take credit for?

Where is the space
this week for
contemplation?

DAY(S):
TIME:
ACTIVITY:

DATE
QUARTERLY FOCUS:

WEEKLY SNAPSHOT:

MON	TUE	WED	THU	FRI	SAT	SUN

IT'S OKAY TO DO THINGS 80%

TODAY'S OBJECTIVES

1 PROJECT / GOAL	SPECIFIC **TASKS**

2 PROJECT / GOAL	SPECIFIC **TASKS**

3 PROJECT / GOAL	SPECIFIC **TASKS**

Which tasks are not necessary for me to do?
Which tasks can be delegated?"

_____

_____

_____

_____

What does success look like to me? If I step back from the
expectations of others, what do I actually want to do today?

_____

_____

YESTERDAY'S WIN:

**M O T I V E S
C H E C K**

What can I do
today and not
take credit for?

Where is the space
this week for
contemplation?

DAY(S):
TIME:
ACTIVITY:

DATE
QUARTERLY FOCUS:

WEEKLY SNAPSHOT:

MON	TUE	WED	THU	FRI	SAT	SUN

IT'S OKAY TO DO THINGS 80%

T O D A Y ' S
O B J E C T I V E S

1 PROJECT / GOAL	SPECIFIC TASKS

2 PROJECT / GOAL	SPECIFIC TASKS

3 PROJECT / GOAL	SPECIFIC TASKS

Which tasks are not necessary for me to do?
Which tasks can be delegated?"

What does success look like to me? If I step back from the
expectations of others, what do I actually want to do today?

YESTERDAY'S WIN:

M O T I V E S
C H E C K

What can I do
today and not
take credit for?

Where is the space
this week for
contemplation?

DAY(S):
TIME:
ACTIVITY:

DATE
QUARTERLY FOCUS:

YOU ARE MORE THAN WHAT YOU DO
You are LOVED for **who you are** not what you do

WEEKLY SNAPSHOT:

MON	TUE	WED	THU	FRI	SAT	SUN

IT'S OKAY TO DO THINGS 80%

TODAY'S OBJECTIVES

1 PROJECT / GOAL	SPECIFIC **TASKS**

2 PROJECT / GOAL	SPECIFIC **TASKS**

3 PROJECT / GOAL	SPECIFIC **TASKS**

Which tasks are not necessary for me to do?
Which tasks can be delegated?"

_____

_____

_____

What does success look like to me? If I step back from the
expectations of others, what do I actually want to do today?

_____

_____

YESTERDAY'S WIN:

M O T I V E S
C H E C K

What can I do
today and not
take credit for?

Where is the space
this week for
contemplation?

DAY(S):
TIME:
ACTIVITY:

DATE
QUARTERLY FOCUS:

YOU ARE MORE THAN WHAT YOU DO
You are LOVED for **who you are** not what you do

WEEKLY SNAPSHOT:

MON	TUE	WED	THU	FRI	SAT	SUN

IT'S OKAY TO DO THINGS 80%

T O D A Y ' S
O B J E C T I V E S

1 PROJECT / GOAL	SPECIFIC **TASKS**

2 PROJECT / GOAL	SPECIFIC **TASKS**

3 PROJECT / GOAL	SPECIFIC **TASKS**

Which tasks are not necessary for me to do?
Which tasks can be delegated?"

_____

_____

_____

What does success look like to me? If I step back from the
expectations of others, what do I actually want to do today?

_____

_____

YESTERDAY'S WIN:

M O T I V E S
C H E C K

What can I do
today and not
take credit for?

Where is the space
this week for
contemplation?

DAY(S):
TIME:
ACTIVITY:

DATE
QUARTERLY FOCUS:

YOU ARE MORE THAN WHAT YOU DO
You are LOVED for **who you are** not what you do

WEEKLY SNAPSHOT:

MON	TUE	WED	THU	FRI	SAT	SUN

IT'S OKAY TO DO THINGS 80%

TODAY'S OBJECTIVES

1 PROJECT / GOAL	SPECIFIC **TASKS**

2 PROJECT / GOAL	SPECIFIC **TASKS**

3 PROJECT / GOAL	SPECIFIC **TASKS**

Which tasks are not necessary for me to do?
Which tasks can be delegated?"

_____
_____
_____
_____

What does success look like to me? If I step back from the
expectations of others, what do I actually want to do today?

_____
_____

YESTERDAY'S WIN:

M O T I V E S
C H E C K

What can I do
today and not
take credit for?

Where is the space
this week for
contemplation?

DAY(S):
TIME:
ACTIVITY:

DATE

QUARTERLY FOCUS:

YOU ARE MORE THAN WHAT YOU DO
You are LOVED for **who you are** not what you do

WEEKLY SNAPSHOT:

MON	TUE	WED	THU	FRI	SAT	SUN

IT'S OKAY TO DO THINGS 80%

TODAY'S OBJECTIVES

1 PROJECT / GOAL — SPECIFIC **TASKS**

2 PROJECT / GOAL — SPECIFIC **TASKS**

3 PROJECT / GOAL — SPECIFIC **TASKS**

Which tasks are not necessary for me to do?
Which tasks can be delegated?"

What does success look like to me? If I step back from the expectations of others, what do I actually want to do today?

YESTERDAY'S WIN:

MOTIVES CHECK

What can I do today and not take credit for?

Where is the space this week for contemplation?

DAY(S):
TIME:
ACTIVITY:

DATE
QUARTERLY FOCUS:

WEEKLY SNAPSHOT:

MON	TUE	WED	THU	FRI	SAT	SUN

IT'S   OKAY   TO   DO   THINGS   80%

TODAY'S OBJECTIVES

1 **PROJECT** / GOAL	SPECIFIC **TASKS**

2 **PROJECT** / GOAL	SPECIFIC **TASKS**

3 **PROJECT** / GOAL	SPECIFIC **TASKS**

Which tasks are not necessary for me to do?
Which tasks can be delegated?"

_____

_____

_____

_____

What does success look like to me? If I step back from the
expectations of others, what do I actually want to do today?

_____

_____

YESTERDAY'S WIN:

**M O T I V E S
C H E C K**

What can I do
today and not
take credit for?

Where is the space
this week for
contemplation?

DAY(S):
TIME:
ACTIVITY:

DATE

QUARTERLY FOCUS:

YOU ARE MORE THAN WHAT YOU DO
You are LOVED for **who you are** not what you do

WEEKLY SNAPSHOT:

MON	TUE	WED	THU	FRI	SAT	SUN

IT'S OKAY TO DO THINGS 80%

TODAY'S OBJECTIVES

1 PROJECT / GOAL	SPECIFIC **TASKS**

2 PROJECT / GOAL	SPECIFIC **TASKS**

3 PROJECT / GOAL	SPECIFIC **TASKS**

Which tasks are not necessary for me to do?
Which tasks can be delegated?"

_____

_____

_____

What does success look like to me? If I step back from the
expectations of others, what do I actually want to do today?

_____

_____

YESTERDAY'S WIN:

MOTIVES CHECK

What can I do
today and not
take credit for?

Where is the space
this week for
contemplation?

DAY(S):
TIME:
ACTIVITY:

DATE
QUARTERLY FOCUS:

YOU ARE MORE THAN WHAT YOU DO
You are LOVED for **who you are** not what you do

WEEKLY SNAPSHOT:

MON	TUE	WED	THU	FRI	SAT	SUN

IT'S OKAY TO DO THINGS 80%

TODAY'S OBJECTIVES

1 PROJECT / GOAL	SPECIFIC **TASKS**

2 PROJECT / GOAL	SPECIFIC **TASKS**

3 PROJECT / GOAL	SPECIFIC **TASKS**

Which tasks are not necessary for me to do?
Which tasks can be delegated?"

_____

_____

_____

_____

What does success look like to me? If I step back from the
expectations of others, what do I actually want to do today?

_____

_____

YESTERDAY'S WIN:

M O T I V E S
C H E C K

What can I do
today and not
take credit for?

Where is the space
this week for
contemplation?

DAY(S):
TIME:
ACTIVITY:

DATE

QUARTERLY FOCUS:

WEEKLY SNAPSHOT:

MON	TUE	WED	THU	FRI	SAT	SUN

IT'S   OKAY   TO   DO   THINGS   80%

T O D A Y ' S
O B J E C T I V E S

1 PROJECT / GOAL

SPECIFIC **TASKS**

2 PROJECT / GOAL

SPECIFIC **TASKS**

3 PROJECT / GOAL

SPECIFIC **TASKS**

Which tasks are not necessary for me to do?
Which tasks can be delegated?"

_____

_____

_____

What does success look like to me? If I step back from the
expectations of others, what do I actually want to do today?

_____

_____

YESTERDAY'S WIN:

M O T I V E S
C   H   E   C   K

What can I do
today and not
take credit for?

Where is the space
this week for
contemplation?

DAY(S):
TIME:
ACTIVITY:

DATE
QUARTERLY FOCUS:

WEEKLY SNAPSHOT:

MON	TUE	WED	THU	FRI	SAT	SUN

IT'S OKAY TO DO THINGS 80%

TODAY'S OBJECTIVES

1 PROJECT / GOAL	SPECIFIC **TASKS**

2 PROJECT / GOAL	SPECIFIC **TASKS**

3 PROJECT / GOAL	SPECIFIC **TASKS**

Which tasks are not necessary for me to do?
Which tasks can be delegated?"

_____

_____

_____

_____

What does success look like to me? If I step back from the
expectations of others, what do I actually want to do today?

_____

_____

YESTERDAY'S WIN:

**M O T I V E S
C H E C K**

What can I do
today and not
take credit for?

Where is the space
this week for
contemplation?

DAY(S):
TIME:
ACTIVITY:

DATE
QUARTERLY FOCUS:

WEEKLY SNAPSHOT:

MON	TUE	WED	THU	FRI	SAT	SUN

IT'S OKAY TO DO THINGS 8 0 %

T O D A Y ' S
O B J E C T I V E S

1 PROJECT / GOAL	SPECIFIC TASKS

2 PROJECT / GOAL	SPECIFIC TASKS

3 PROJECT / GOAL	SPECIFIC TASKS

Which tasks are not necessary for me to do?
Which tasks can be delegated?"

_____

_____

_____

What does success look like to me? If I step back from the
expectations of others, what do I actually want to do today?

_____

_____

YESTERDAY'S WIN:

M O T I V E S
C H E C K

What can I do
today and not
take credit for?

Where is the space
this week for
contemplation?

DAY(S):
TIME:
ACTIVITY:

DATE
QUARTERLY FOCUS:

YOU ARE MORE THAN WHAT YOU DO
You are LOVED for **who you are** not what you do

WEEKLY SNAPSHOT:

MON	TUE	WED	THU	FRI	SAT	SUN

IT'S OKAY TO DO THINGS 80%

TODAY'S OBJECTIVES

1 PROJECT / GOAL	SPECIFIC **TASKS**

2 PROJECT / GOAL	SPECIFIC **TASKS**

3 PROJECT / GOAL	SPECIFIC **TASKS**

Which tasks are not necessary for me to do?
Which tasks can be delegated?"

_____

_____

_____

_____

What does success look like to me? If I step back from the
expectations of others, what do I actually want to do today?

_____

_____

YESTERDAY'S WIN:

M O T I V E S
C H E C K

What can I do
today and not
take credit for?

Where is the space
this week for
contemplation?

DAY(S):
TIME:
ACTIVITY:

DATE
QUARTERLY FOCUS:

WEEKLY SNAPSHOT:

MON	TUE	WED	THU	FRI	SAT	SUN

IT'S OKAY TO DO THINGS 80%

T O D A Y ' S
O B J E C T I V E S

1 **PROJECT** / GOAL	SPECIFIC **TASKS**

2 **PROJECT** / GOAL	SPECIFIC **TASKS**

3 **PROJECT** / GOAL	SPECIFIC **TASKS**

Which tasks are not necessary for me to do?
Which tasks can be delegated?"

_____

_____

_____

What does success look like to me? If I step back from the
expectations of others, what do I actually want to do today?

_____

_____

YESTERDAY'S WIN:

M O T I V E S
C H E C K

What can I do
today and not
take credit for?

Where is the space
this week for
contemplation?

DAY(S):
TIME:
ACTIVITY:

DATE
QUARTERLY FOCUS:

WEEKLY SNAPSHOT:

MON	TUE	WED	THU	FRI	SAT	SUN

IT'S OKAY TO DO THINGS 8 0 %

TODAY'S OBJECTIVES

1 **PROJECT** / GOAL	SPECIFIC **TASKS**

2 **PROJECT** / GOAL	SPECIFIC **TASKS**

3 **PROJECT** / GOAL	SPECIFIC **TASKS**

Which tasks are not necessary for me to do?
Which tasks can be delegated?"

_____

_____

_____

What does success look like to me? If I step back from the
expectations of others, what do I actually want to do today?

_____

_____

YESTERDAY'S WIN:

**M O T I V E S
C H E C K**

What can I do
today and not
take credit for?

Where is the space
this week for
contemplation?

DAY(S):
TIME:
ACTIVITY:

DATE
QUARTERLY FOCUS:

YOU ARE MORE THAN WHAT YOU DO
You are LOVED for **who you are** not what you do

WEEKLY SNAPSHOT:

MON	TUE	WED	THU	FRI	SAT	SUN

IT'S   OKAY   TO   DO   THINGS   **80%**

T O D A Y ' S
O B J E C T I V E S

1 PROJECT / GOAL | SPECIFIC **TASKS**

2 PROJECT / GOAL | SPECIFIC **TASKS**

3 PROJECT / GOAL | SPECIFIC **TASKS**

Which tasks are not necessary for me to do?
Which tasks can be delegated?"

_____

_____

_____

What does success look like to me? If I step back from the
expectations of others, what do I actually want to do today?

_____

_____

YESTERDAY'S WIN:

M O T I V E S
C H E C K

What can I do
today and not
take credit for?

Where is the space
this week for
contemplation?

DAY(S):
TIME:
ACTIVITY:

DATE
QUARTERLY FOCUS:

YOU ARE MORE THAN WHAT YOU DO
You are LOVED for **who you are** not what you do

WEEKLY SNAPSHOT:

MON	TUE	WED	THU	FRI	SAT	SUN

IT'S OKAY TO DO THINGS 80%

TODAY'S OBJECTIVES

1 PROJECT / GOAL	SPECIFIC **TASKS**

2 PROJECT / GOAL	SPECIFIC **TASKS**

3 PROJECT / GOAL	SPECIFIC **TASKS**

Which tasks are not necessary for me to do?
Which tasks can be delegated?"

_____

_____

_____

What does success look like to me? If I step back from the
expectations of others, what do I actually want to do today?

_____

_____

YESTERDAY'S WIN:

M O T I V E S
C H E C K

What can I do
today and not
take credit for?

Where is the space
this week for
contemplation?

DAY(S):
TIME:
ACTIVITY:

DATE
QUARTERLY FOCUS:

WEEKLY SNAPSHOT:

MON	TUE	WED	THU	FRI	SAT	SUN

IT'S OKAY TO DO THINGS 80%

TODAY'S OBJECTIVES

1 PROJECT / GOAL	SPECIFIC **TASKS**

2 PROJECT / GOAL	SPECIFIC **TASKS**

3 PROJECT / GOAL	SPECIFIC **TASKS**

Which tasks are not necessary for me to do?
Which tasks can be delegated?"

_____

_____

_____

What does success look like to me? If I step back from the
expectations of others, what do I actually want to do today?

_____

_____

YESTERDAY'S WIN:

MOTIVES CHECK

What can I do
today and not
take credit for?

Where is the space
this week for
contemplation?

DAY(S):
TIME:
ACTIVITY:

DATE
QUARTERLY FOCUS:

WEEKLY SNAPSHOT:

YOU ARE MORE THAN WHAT YOU DO
You are LOVED for **who you are** not what you do

MON	TUE	WED	THU	FRI	SAT	SUN

IT'S OKAY TO DO THINGS 80%

TODAY'S OBJECTIVES

1 PROJECT / GOAL

SPECIFIC **TASKS**

2 PROJECT / GOAL

SPECIFIC **TASKS**

3 PROJECT / GOAL

SPECIFIC **TASKS**

Which tasks are not necessary for me to do?
Which tasks can be delegated?"

_____

_____

_____

What does success look like to me? If I step back from the
expectations of others, what do I actually want to do today?

_____

_____

YESTERDAY'S WIN:

**M O T I V E S
C H E C K**

What can I do
today and not
take credit for?

Where is the space
this week for
contemplation?

DAY(S):
TIME:
ACTIVITY:

DATE
QUARTERLY FOCUS:

WEEKLY SNAPSHOT:

MON	TUE	WED	THU	FRI	SAT	SUN

IT'S OKAY TO DO THINGS 80%

T O D A Y ' S
O B J E C T I V E S

1 PROJECT / GOAL	SPECIFIC **TASKS**

2 PROJECT / GOAL	SPECIFIC **TASKS**

3 PROJECT / GOAL	SPECIFIC **TASKS**

Which tasks are not necessary for me to do?
Which tasks can be delegated?"

_____

_____

_____

What does success look like to me? If I step back from the
expectations of others, what do I actually want to do today?

_____

_____

YESTERDAY'S WIN:

M O T I V E S
C H E C K

What can I do
today and not
take credit for?

Where is the space
this week for
contemplation?

DAY(S):
TIME:
ACTIVITY:

DATE
QUARTERLY FOCUS:

WEEKLY SNAPSHOT:

MON	TUE	WED	THU	FRI	SAT	SUN

IT'S OKAY TO DO THINGS **8 0 %**

TODAY'S OBJECTIVES

1 **PROJECT /** GOAL	SPECIFIC **TASKS**

2 **PROJECT /** GOAL	SPECIFIC **TASKS**

3 **PROJECT /** GOAL	SPECIFIC **TASKS**

Which tasks are not necessary for me to do?
Which tasks can be delegated?"

_____

_____

_____

What does success look like to me? If I step back from the
expectations of others, what do I actually want to do today?

_____

_____

YESTERDAY'S WIN:

M O T I V E S
C H E C K

What can I do
today and not
take credit for?

Where is the space
this week for
contemplation?

DAY(S):
TIME:
ACTIVITY:

DATE
QUARTERLY FOCUS:

YOU ARE MORE THAN WHAT YOU DO
You are LOVED for **who you are** not what you do

WEEKLY SNAPSHOT:

MON	TUE	WED	THU	FRI	SAT	SUN

IT'S   OKAY   TO   DO   THINGS   **80%**

T O D A Y ' S
O B J E C T I V E S

1 PROJECT / GOAL	SPECIFIC **TASKS**

2 PROJECT / GOAL	SPECIFIC **TASKS**

3 PROJECT / GOAL	SPECIFIC **TASKS**

Which tasks are not necessary for me to do?
Which tasks can be delegated?"

_____

_____

_____

What does success look like to me? If I step back from the
expectations of others, what do I actually want to do today?

_____

_____

YESTERDAY'S WIN:

M O T I V E S
C H E C K

What can I do
today and not
take credit for?

Where is the space
this week for
contemplation?

DAY(S):
TIME:
ACTIVITY:

DATE
QUARTERLY FOCUS:

WEEKLY SNAPSHOT:

MON	TUE	WED	THU	FRI	SAT	SUN

IT'S OKAY TO DO THINGS 80%

TODAY'S OBJECTIVES

1 **PROJECT** / GOAL	SPECIFIC **TASKS**

2 **PROJECT** / GOAL	SPECIFIC **TASKS**

3 **PROJECT** / GOAL	SPECIFIC **TASKS**

Which tasks are not necessary for me to do?
Which tasks can be delegated?"

_____

_____

_____

What does success look like to me? If I step back from the
expectations of others, what do I actually want to do today?

_____

YESTERDAY'S WIN:

M O T I V E S
C H E C K

What can I do
today and not
take credit for?

Where is the space
this week for
contemplation?

DAY(S):
TIME:
ACTIVITY:

DATE
QUARTERLY FOCUS:

WEEKLY SNAPSHOT:

MON	TUE	WED	THU	FRI	SAT	SUN

IT'S OKAY TO DO THINGS 80%

T O D A Y ' S
O B J E C T I V E S

1 PROJECT / GOAL	SPECIFIC **TASKS**

2 PROJECT / GOAL	SPECIFIC **TASKS**

3 PROJECT / GOAL	SPECIFIC **TASKS**

Which tasks are not necessary for me to do?
Which tasks can be delegated?

_____

_____

_____

What does success look like to me? If I step back from the
expectations of others, what do I actually want to do today?

_____

_____

YESTERDAY'S WIN:

M O T I V E S
C H E C K

What can I do
today and not
take credit for?

Where is the space
this week for
contemplation?

DAY(S):
TIME:
ACTIVITY:

DATE
QUARTERLY FOCUS:

WEEKLY SNAPSHOT:

MON	TUE	WED	THU	FRI	SAT	SUN

IT'S OKAY TO DO THINGS 80%

TODAY'S OBJECTIVES

1 PROJECT / GOAL	SPECIFIC **TASKS**

2 PROJECT / GOAL	SPECIFIC **TASKS**

3 PROJECT / GOAL	SPECIFIC **TASKS**

Which tasks are not necessary for me to do?
Which tasks can be delegated?"

_____

_____

_____

_____

What does success look like to me? If I step back from the
expectations of others, what do I actually want to do today?

_____

_____

YESTERDAY'S WIN:

M O T I V E S
C H E C K

What can I do
today and not
take credit for?

Where is the space
this week for
contemplation?

DAY(S):
TIME:
ACTIVITY:

DATE
QUARTERLY FOCUS:

WEEKLY SNAPSHOT:

MON	TUE	WED	THU	FRI	SAT	SUN

IT'S OKAY TO DO THINGS 80%

T O D A Y ' S
O B J E C T I V E S

1 **PROJECT** / GOAL		SPECIFIC **TASKS**

2 **PROJECT** / GOAL		SPECIFIC **TASKS**

3 **PROJECT** / GOAL		SPECIFIC **TASKS**

Which tasks are not necessary for me to do?
Which tasks can be delegated?"

_____

_____

_____

_____

What does success look like to me? If I step back from the
expectations of others, what do I actually want to do today?

_____

_____

YESTERDAY'S WIN:

M O T I V E S
C H E C K

What can I do
today and not
take credit for?

Where is the space
this week for
contemplation?

DAY(S):
TIME:
ACTIVITY:

DATE
QUARTERLY FOCUS:

YOU ARE MORE THAN WHAT YOU DO
You are LOVED for **who you are** not what you do

WEEKLY SNAPSHOT:

MON	TUE	WED	THU	FRI	SAT	SUN

IT'S OKAY TO DO THINGS 80%

TODAY'S OBJECTIVES

1 **PROJECT / GOAL**	SPECIFIC **TASKS**

2 **PROJECT / GOAL**	SPECIFIC **TASKS**

3 **PROJECT / GOAL**	SPECIFIC **TASKS**

Which tasks are not necessary for me to do?
Which tasks can be delegated?

_____

_____

_____

What does success look like to me? If I step back from the
expectations of others, what do I actually want to do today?

_____

_____

YESTERDAY'S WIN:

**MOTIVES
CHECK**

What can I do
today and not
take credit for?

Where is the space
this week for
contemplation?

DAY(S):
TIME:
ACTIVITY:

DATE
QUARTERLY FOCUS:

YOU ARE MORE THAN WHAT YOU DO
You are LOVED for **who you are** not what you do

WEEKLY SNAPSHOT:

MON	TUE	WED	THU	FRI	SAT	SUN

IT'S OKAY TO DO THINGS 80%

TODAY'S OBJECTIVES

1 PROJECT / GOAL

SPECIFIC **TASKS**

2 PROJECT / GOAL

SPECIFIC **TASKS**

3 PROJECT / GOAL

SPECIFIC **TASKS**

Which tasks are not necessary for me to do?
Which tasks can be delegated?"

_____

_____

_____

_____

What does success look like to me? If I step back from the
expectations of others, what do I actually want to do today?

_____

_____

YESTERDAY'S WIN:

MOTIVES CHECK

What can I do
today and not
take credit for?

Where is the space
this week for
contemplation?

DAY(S):
TIME:
ACTIVITY:

DATE
QUARTERLY FOCUS:

WEEKLY SNAPSHOT:

MON	TUE	WED	THU	FRI	SAT	SUN

IT'S OKAY TO DO THINGS 80%

TODAY'S OBJECTIVES

1 **PROJECT** / GOAL	SPECIFIC **TASKS**

2 **PROJECT** / GOAL	SPECIFIC **TASKS**

3 **PROJECT** / GOAL	SPECIFIC **TASKS**

Which tasks are not necessary for me to do?
Which tasks can be delegated?"

_____

_____

_____

What does success look like to me? If I step back from the
expectations of others, what do I actually want to do today?

_____

_____

YESTERDAY'S WIN:

M O T I V E S
C H E C K

What can I do
today and not
take credit for?

Where is the space
this week for
contemplation?

DAY(S):
TIME:
ACTIVITY:

DATE
QUARTERLY FOCUS:

WEEKLY SNAPSHOT:

MON	TUE	WED	THU	FRI	SAT	SUN

IT'S OKAY TO DO THINGS 80%

TODAY'S OBJECTIVES

1 PROJECT / GOAL	SPECIFIC TASKS

2 PROJECT / GOAL	SPECIFIC TASKS

3 PROJECT / GOAL	SPECIFIC TASKS

Which tasks are not necessary for me to do?
Which tasks can be delegated?"

_____

_____

_____

What does success look like to me? If I step back from the expectations of others, what do I actually want to do today?

_____

_____

YESTERDAY'S WIN:

YOU ARE MORE THAN WHAT YOU DO
You are LOVED for **who you are** not what you do

MOTIVES CHECK

What can I do today and not take credit for?

Where is the space this week for contemplation?

DAY(S):
TIME:
ACTIVITY:

DATE
QUARTERLY FOCUS:

YOU ARE MORE THAN WHAT YOU DO
You are LOVED for **who you are** not what you do

WEEKLY SNAPSHOT:

MON	TUE	WED	THU	FRI	SAT	SUN

IT'S OKAY TO DO THINGS 80%

TODAY'S OBJECTIVES

1 **PROJECT** / GOAL		SPECIFIC **TASKS**

2 **PROJECT** / GOAL		SPECIFIC **TASKS**

3 **PROJECT** / GOAL		SPECIFIC **TASKS**

Which tasks are not necessary for me to do?
Which tasks can be delegated?"

_____

_____

_____

What does success look like to me? If I step back from the
expectations of others, what do I actually want to do today?

_____

_____

YESTERDAY'S WIN:

**M O T I V E S
C H E C K**

What can I do
today and not
take credit for?

Where is the space
this week for
contemplation?

DAY(S):
TIME:
ACTIVITY:

DATE
QUARTERLY FOCUS:

WEEKLY SNAPSHOT:

MON	TUE	WED	THU	FRI	SAT	SUN

IT'S OKAY TO DO THINGS **80%**

T O D A Y ' S
O B J E C T I V E S

1 PROJECT / GOAL	SPECIFIC **TASKS**

2 PROJECT / GOAL	SPECIFIC **TASKS**

3 PROJECT / GOAL	SPECIFIC **TASKS**

Which tasks are not necessary for me to do?
Which tasks can be delegated?"

_____

_____

_____

_____

What does success look like to me? If I step back from the
expectations of others, what do I actually want to do today?

_____

_____

YESTERDAY'S WIN:

M O T I V E S
C H E C K

What can I do
today and not
take credit for?

Where is the space
this week for
contemplation?

DAY(S):
TIME:
ACTIVITY:

DATE
QUARTERLY FOCUS:

YOU ARE MORE THAN WHAT YOU DO
You are LOVED for **who you are** not what you do

WEEKLY SNAPSHOT:

MON	TUE	WED	THU	FRI	SAT	SUN

IT'S OKAY TO DO THINGS 80%

TODAY'S OBJECTIVES

1 PROJECT / GOAL	SPECIFIC **TASKS**

2 PROJECT / GOAL	SPECIFIC **TASKS**

3 PROJECT / GOAL	SPECIFIC **TASKS**

Which tasks are not necessary for me to do?
Which tasks can be delegated?

_____

_____

_____

What does success look like to me? If I step back from the
expectations of others, what do I actually want to do today?

_____

_____

YESTERDAY'S WIN:

MOTIVES CHECK

What can I do
today and not
take credit for?

Where is the space
this week for
contemplation?

DAY(S):
TIME:
ACTIVITY:

DATE
QUARTERLY FOCUS:

YOU ARE MORE THAN WHAT YOU DO
You are LOVED for **who you are** not what you do

WEEKLY SNAPSHOT:

MON	TUE	WED	THU	FRI	SAT	SUN

IT'S OKAY TO DO THINGS 80%

TODAY'S
OBJECTIVES

1 PROJECT / GOAL

SPECIFIC **TASKS**

2 PROJECT / GOAL

SPECIFIC **TASKS**

3 PROJECT / GOAL

SPECIFIC **TASKS**

Which tasks are not necessary for me to do?
Which tasks can be delegated?"

_____

_____

_____

What does success look like to me? If I step back from the
expectations of others, what do I actually want to do today?

_____

_____

YESTERDAY'S WIN:

MOTIVES
CHECK

What can I do
today and not
take credit for?

Where is the space
this week for
contemplation?

DAY(S):
TIME:
ACTIVITY:

DATE
QUARTERLY FOCUS:

WEEKLY SNAPSHOT:

MON	TUE	WED	THU	FRI	SAT	SUN

IT'S OKAY TO DO THINGS 80%   **TODAY'S** OBJECTIVES

1 PROJECT / GOAL	SPECIFIC **TASKS**

2 PROJECT / GOAL	SPECIFIC **TASKS**

3 PROJECT / GOAL	SPECIFIC **TASKS**

Which tasks are not necessary for me to do?
Which tasks can be delegated?"

_____

_____

_____

_____

What does success look like to me? If I step back from the
expectations of others, what do I actually want to do today?

_____

_____

YESTERDAY'S WIN:

**M O T I V E S
C H E C K**

What can I do
today and not
take credit for?

Where is the space
this week for
contemplation?

DAY(S):
TIME:
ACTIVITY:

DATE
QUARTERLY FOCUS:

WEEKLY SNAPSHOT:

MON	TUE	WED	THU	FRI	SAT	SUN

IT'S   OKAY   TO   DO   THINGS   **80%**

T O D A Y ' S
O B J E C T I V E S

1 PROJECT / GOAL	SPECIFIC **TASKS**

2 PROJECT / GOAL	SPECIFIC **TASKS**

3 PROJECT / GOAL	SPECIFIC **TASKS**

Which tasks are not necessary for me to do?
Which tasks can be delegated?"

_____

_____

_____

What does success look like to me? If I step back from the
expectations of others, what do I actually want to do today?

_____

_____

YESTERDAY'S WIN:

M O T I V E S
C H E C K

What can I do
today and not
take credit for?

Where is the space
this week for
contemplation?

DAY(S):
TIME:
ACTIVITY:

DATE
QUARTERLY FOCUS:

WEEKLY SNAPSHOT:

MON	TUE	WED	THU	FRI	SAT	SUN

IT'S OKAY TO DO THINGS 80%

TODAY'S OBJECTIVES

1 **PROJECT** / GOAL	SPECIFIC **TASKS**

2 **PROJECT** / GOAL	SPECIFIC **TASKS**

3 **PROJECT** / GOAL	SPECIFIC **TASKS**

Which tasks are not necessary for me to do?
Which tasks can be delegated?"

_____

_____

_____

What does success look like to me? If I step back from the
expectations of others, what do I actually want to do today?

_____

_____

YESTERDAY'S WIN:

**M O T I V E S
C H E C K**

What can I do
today and not
take credit for?

Where is the space
this week for
contemplation?

DAY(S):
TIME:
ACTIVITY:

DATE
QUARTERLY FOCUS:

WEEKLY SNAPSHOT:

MON	TUE	WED	THU	FRI	SAT	SUN

IT'S OKAY TO DO THINGS 80%

TODAY'S OBJECTIVES

1 PROJECT / GOAL

SPECIFIC **TASKS**

2 PROJECT / GOAL

SPECIFIC **TASKS**

3 PROJECT / GOAL

SPECIFIC **TASKS**

Which tasks are not necessary for me to do?
Which tasks can be delegated?"

_____

_____

_____

What does success look like to me? If I step back from the expectations of others, what do I actually want to do today?

_____

_____

YESTERDAY'S WIN:

MOTIVES CHECK

What can I do today and not take credit for?

Where is the space this week for contemplation?

DAY(S):
TIME:
ACTIVITY:

DATE
QUARTERLY FOCUS:

YOU ARE MORE THAN WHAT YOU DO
You are LOVED for **who you are** not what you do

WEEKLY SNAPSHOT:

MON	TUE	WED	THU	FRI	SAT	SUN

IT'S OKAY TO DO THINGS 80%

TODAY'S OBJECTIVES

1 PROJECT / GOAL	SPECIFIC **TASKS**

2 PROJECT / GOAL	SPECIFIC **TASKS**

3 PROJECT / GOAL	SPECIFIC **TASKS**

Which tasks are not necessary for me to do?
Which tasks can be delegated?

MOTIVES CHECK

What can I do today and not take credit for?

What does success look like to me? If I step back from the expectations of others, what do I actually want to do today?

Where is the space this week for contemplation?

DAY(S):
TIME:
ACTIVITY:

YESTERDAY'S WIN:

DATE
QUARTERLY FOCUS:

YOU ARE MORE THAN WHAT YOU DO
You are LOVED for **who you are** not what you do

WEEKLY SNAPSHOT:

MON	TUE	WED	THU	FRI	SAT	SUN

IT'S OKAY TO DO THINGS 80%

TODAY'S OBJECTIVES

1 PROJECT / GOAL

SPECIFIC **TASKS**

2 PROJECT / GOAL

SPECIFIC **TASKS**

3 PROJECT / GOAL

SPECIFIC **TASKS**

Which tasks are not necessary for me to do?
Which tasks can be delegated?"

_____

_____

_____

What does success look like to me? If I step back from the
expectations of others, what do I actually want to do today?

_____

_____

YESTERDAY'S WIN:

MOTIVES CHECK

What can I do
today and not
take credit for?

Where is the space
this week for
contemplation?

DAY(S):
TIME:
ACTIVITY:

DATE
QUARTERLY FOCUS:

YOU ARE MORE THAN WHAT YOU DO
You are LOVED for **who you are** not what you do

WEEKLY SNAPSHOT:

MON	TUE	WED	THU	FRI	SAT	SUN

IT'S OKAY TO DO THINGS 80%

TODAY'S OBJECTIVES

1 PROJECT / GOAL	SPECIFIC **TASKS**

2 PROJECT / GOAL	SPECIFIC **TASKS**

3 PROJECT / GOAL	SPECIFIC **TASKS**

Which tasks are not necessary for me to do?
Which tasks can be delegated?"

_____

_____

_____

What does success look like to me? If I step back from the
expectations of others, what do I actually want to do today?

_____

_____

YESTERDAY'S WIN:

M O T I V E S
C H E C K

What can I do
today and not
take credit for?

Where is the space
this week for
contemplation?

DAY(S):
TIME:
ACTIVITY:

DATE
QUARTERLY FOCUS:

YOU ARE MORE THAN WHAT YOU DO
You are LOVED for **who you are** not what you do

WEEKLY SNAPSHOT:

MON	TUE	WED	THU	FRI	SAT	SUN

IT'S OKAY TO DO THINGS 80%

TODAY'S OBJECTIVES

1 **PROJECT** / GOAL	SPECIFIC **TASKS**

2 **PROJECT** / GOAL	SPECIFIC **TASKS**

3 **PROJECT** / GOAL	SPECIFIC **TASKS**

Which tasks are not necessary for me to do?
Which tasks can be delegated?

What does success look like to me? If I step back from the
expectations of others, what do I actually want to do today?

YESTERDAY'S WIN:

MOTIVES CHECK

What can I do
today and not
take credit for?

Where is the space
this week for
contemplation?

DAY(S):
TIME:
ACTIVITY:

DATE
QUARTERLY FOCUS:

YOU ARE MORE THAN WHAT YOU DO
You are LOVED for **who you are** not what you do

WEEKLY SNAPSHOT:

MON	TUE	WED	THU	FRI	SAT	SUN

IT'S OKAY TO DO THINGS **80%**

TODAY'S OBJECTIVES

1 PROJECT / GOAL

SPECIFIC **TASKS**

2 PROJECT / GOAL

SPECIFIC **TASKS**

3 PROJECT / GOAL

SPECIFIC **TASKS**

Which tasks are not necessary for me to do?
Which tasks can be delegated?"

_____

_____

_____

_____

What does success look like to me? If I step back from the
expectations of others, what do I actually want to do today?

_____

_____

YESTERDAY'S WIN:

M O T I V E S
C H E C K

What can I do
today and not
take credit for?

Where is the space
this week for
contemplation?

DAY(S):
TIME:
ACTIVITY:

DATE
QUARTERLY FOCUS:

WEEKLY SNAPSHOT:

MON	TUE	WED	THU	FRI	SAT	SUN

IT'S OKAY TO DO THINGS 80%

TODAY'S OBJECTIVES

1 **PROJECT** / GOAL	SPECIFIC **TASKS**

2 **PROJECT** / GOAL	SPECIFIC **TASKS**

3 **PROJECT** / GOAL	SPECIFIC **TASKS**

Which tasks are not necessary for me to do?
Which tasks can be delegated?"

_____

_____

_____

_____

What does success look like to me? If I step back from the
expectations of others, what do I actually want to do today?

_____

_____

YESTERDAY'S WIN:

MOTIVES CHECK

What can I do
today and not
take credit for?

Where is the space
this week for
contemplation?

DAY(S):
TIME:
ACTIVITY:

DATE
QUARTERLY FOCUS:

WEEKLY SNAPSHOT:

MON	TUE	WED	THU	FRI	SAT	SUN

IT'S OKAY TO DO THINGS **80%** **TODAY'S** OBJECTIVES

1 PROJECT / GOAL	SPECIFIC **TASKS**

2 PROJECT / GOAL	SPECIFIC **TASKS**

3 PROJECT / GOAL	SPECIFIC **TASKS**

Which tasks are not necessary for me to do?
Which tasks can be delegated?

_____

_____

_____

What does success look like to me? If I step back from the
expectations of others, what do I actually want to do today?

_____

_____

YESTERDAY'S WIN:

**M O T I V E S
C H E C K**

What can I do
today and not
take credit for?

Where is the space
this week for
contemplation?

DAY(S):
TIME:
ACTIVITY:

DATE
QUARTERLY FOCUS:

YOU ARE MORE THAN WHAT YOU DO
You are LOVED for **who you are** not what you do

MON	TUE	WED	THU	FRI	SAT	SUN

IT'S OKAY TO DO THINGS 80%

T O D A Y ' S
O B J E C T I V E S

1 PROJECT / GOAL

SPECIFIC **TASKS**

2 PROJECT / GOAL

SPECIFIC **TASKS**

3 PROJECT / GOAL

SPECIFIC **TASKS**

Which tasks are not necessary for me to do?
Which tasks can be delegated?"

_____

_____

_____

What does success look like to me? If I step back from the
expectations of others, what do I actually want to do today?

_____

_____

YESTERDAY'S WIN:

M O T I V E S
C H E C K

What can I do
today and not
take credit for?

Where is the space
this week for
contemplation?

DAY(S):
TIME:
ACTIVITY:

DATE
QUARTERLY FOCUS:

WEEKLY SNAPSHOT:

MON	TUE	WED	THU	FRI	SAT	SUN

IT'S OKAY TO DO THINGS 80%

TODAY'S OBJECTIVES

1 **PROJECT / GOAL**	SPECIFIC **TASKS**

2 **PROJECT / GOAL**	SPECIFIC **TASKS**

3 **PROJECT / GOAL**	SPECIFIC **TASKS**

Which tasks are not necessary for me to do?
Which tasks can be delegated?"

What does success look like to me? If I step back from the
expectations of others, what do I actually want to do today?

YESTERDAY'S WIN:

**M O T I V E S
C H E C K**

What can I do
today and not
take credit for?

Where is the space
this week for
contemplation?

DAY(S):
TIME:
ACTIVITY:

DATE
QUARTERLY FOCUS:

WEEKLY SNAPSHOT:

MON	TUE	WED	THU	FRI	SAT	SUN

IT'S   OKAY   TO   DO   THINGS   **80%**

TODAY'S OBJECTIVES

1 PROJECT / GOAL	SPECIFIC **TASKS**

2 PROJECT / GOAL	SPECIFIC **TASKS**

3 PROJECT / GOAL	SPECIFIC **TASKS**

Which tasks are not necessary for me to do?
Which tasks can be delegated?"

_____

_____

_____

What does success look like to me? If I step back from the
expectations of others, what do I actually want to do today?

_____

_____

YESTERDAY'S WIN:

MOTIVES CHECK

What can I do
today and not
take credit for?

Where is the space
this week for
contemplation?

DAY(S):
TIME:
ACTIVITY:

DATE
QUARTERLY FOCUS:

WEEKLY SNAPSHOT:

MON	TUE	WED	THU	FRI	SAT	SUN

IT'S OKAY TO DO THINGS 80%

TODAY'S OBJECTIVES

1 PROJECT / GOAL	SPECIFIC **TASKS**

2 PROJECT / GOAL	SPECIFIC **TASKS**

3 PROJECT / GOAL	SPECIFIC **TASKS**

Which tasks are not necessary for me to do?
Which tasks can be delegated?"

_____

_____

_____

_____

What does success look like to me? If I step back from the
expectations of others, what do I actually want to do today?

_____

_____

YESTERDAY'S WIN:

M O T I V E S
C H E C K

What can I do
today and not
take credit for?

Where is the space
this week for
contemplation?

DAY(S):
TIME:
ACTIVITY:

DATE

QUARTERLY FOCUS:

WEEKLY SNAPSHOT:

MON	TUE	WED	THU	FRI	SAT	SUN

IT'S OKAY TO DO THINGS 80%

TODAY'S OBJECTIVES

1 PROJECT / GOAL

SPECIFIC **TASKS**

2 PROJECT / GOAL

SPECIFIC **TASKS**

3 PROJECT / GOAL

SPECIFIC **TASKS**

Which tasks are not necessary for me to do?
Which tasks can be delegated?"

_____

_____

_____

What does success look like to me? If I step back from the
expectations of others, what do I actually want to do today?

_____

_____

YESTERDAY'S WIN:

MOTIVES CHECK

What can I do today and not take credit for?

Where is the space this week for contemplation?

DAY(S):
TIME:
ACTIVITY:

DATE
QUARTERLY FOCUS:

YOU ARE MORE THAN WHAT YOU DO
You are LOVED for **who you are** not what you do

WEEKLY SNAPSHOT:

MON	TUE	WED	THU	FRI	SAT	SUN

IT'S OKAY TO DO THINGS 80%

TODAY'S OBJECTIVES

1 PROJECT / GOAL	SPECIFIC TASKS

2 PROJECT / GOAL	SPECIFIC TASKS

3 PROJECT / GOAL	SPECIFIC TASKS

Which tasks are not necessary for me to do?
Which tasks can be delegated?

_____

_____

_____

What does success look like to me? If I step back from the
expectations of others, what do I actually want to do today?

_____

_____

YESTERDAY'S WIN:

MOTIVES CHECK

What can I do
today and not
take credit for?

Where is the space
this week for
contemplation?

DAY(S):
TIME:
ACTIVITY:

DATE
QUARTERLY FOCUS:

YOU ARE MORE THAN WHAT YOU DO
You are LOVED for **who you are** not what you do

WEEKLY SNAPSHOT:

MON	TUE	WED	THU	FRI	SAT	SUN

IT'S OKAY TO DO THINGS **80%**

TODAY'S OBJECTIVES

1 PROJECT / GOAL

SPECIFIC **TASKS**

2 PROJECT / GOAL

SPECIFIC **TASKS**

3 PROJECT / GOAL

SPECIFIC **TASKS**

Which tasks are not necessary for me to do?
Which tasks can be delegated?"

_____

_____

_____

_____

What does success look like to me? If I step back from the
expectations of others, what do I actually want to do today?

_____

_____

YESTERDAY'S WIN:

MOTIVES
CHECK

What can I do
today and not
take credit for?

Where is the space
this week for
contemplation?

DAY(S):
TIME:
ACTIVITY:

DATE
QUARTERLY FOCUS:

YOU ARE MORE THAN WHAT YOU DO
You are LOVED for **who you are** not what you do

WEEKLY SNAPSHOT:

MON	TUE	WED	THU	FRI	SAT	SUN

IT'S OKAY TO DO THINGS 80%

TODAY'S OBJECTIVES

1 PROJECT / GOAL	SPECIFIC **TASKS**

2 PROJECT / GOAL	SPECIFIC **TASKS**

3 PROJECT / GOAL	SPECIFIC **TASKS**

Which tasks are not necessary for me to do?
Which tasks can be delegated?"

_____

_____

_____

What does success look like to me? If I step back from the
expectations of others, what do I actually want to do today?

_____

_____

YESTERDAY'S WIN:

M O T I V E S
C H E C K

What can I do
today and not
take credit for?

Where is the space
this week for
contemplation?

DAY(S):
TIME:
ACTIVITY:

DATE
QUARTERLY FOCUS:

WEEKLY SNAPSHOT:

MON	TUE	WED	THU	FRI	SAT	SUN

IT'S OKAY TO DO THINGS 80%

TODAY'S OBJECTIVES

1 PROJECT / GOAL	SPECIFIC **TASKS**

2 PROJECT / GOAL	SPECIFIC **TASKS**

3 PROJECT / GOAL	SPECIFIC **TASKS**

Which tasks are not necessary for me to do?
Which tasks can be delegated?"

_____

_____

_____

What does success look like to me? If I step back from the
expectations of others, what do I actually want to do today?

_____

_____

YESTERDAY'S WIN:

M O T I V E S
C H E C K

What can I do
today and not
take credit for?

Where is the space
this week for
contemplation?

DAY(S):
TIME:
ACTIVITY:

DATE
QUARTERLY FOCUS:

WEEKLY SNAPSHOT:

MON	TUE	WED	THU	FRI	SAT	SUN

IT'S OKAY TO DO THINGS 80%

TODAY'S OBJECTIVES

1 **PROJECT** / GOAL	SPECIFIC **TASKS**

2 **PROJECT** / GOAL	SPECIFIC **TASKS**

3 **PROJECT** / GOAL	SPECIFIC **TASKS**

Which tasks are not necessary for me to do?
Which tasks can be delegated?"

_____

_____

_____

What does success look like to me? If I step back from the
expectations of others, what do I actually want to do today?

_____

_____

YESTERDAY'S WIN:

**M O T I V E S
C H E C K**

What can I do
today and not
take credit for?

Where is the space
this week for
contemplation?

DAY(S):
TIME:
ACTIVITY:

DATE
QUARTERLY FOCUS:

YOU ARE MORE THAN WHAT YOU DO
You are LOVED for **who you are** not what you do

WEEKLY SNAPSHOT:

MON	TUE	WED	THU	FRI	SAT	SUN

IT'S OKAY TO DO THINGS **80%**

T O D A Y ' S
O B J E C T I V E S

1 PROJECT / GOAL	SPECIFIC **TASKS**

2 PROJECT / GOAL	SPECIFIC **TASKS**

3 PROJECT / GOAL	SPECIFIC **TASKS**

Which tasks are not necessary for me to do?
Which tasks can be delegated?"

_____

_____

_____

What does success look like to me? If I step back from the
expectations of others, what do I actually want to do today?

_____

_____

YESTERDAY'S WIN:

M O T I V E S
C H E C K

What can I do
today and not
take credit for?

Where is the space
this week for
contemplation?

DAY(S):
TIME:
ACTIVITY:

Lightning Source UK Ltd.
Milton Keynes UK
UKHW021450151220
375215UK00001B/24